* WE ARE AMERICA *

Pakistani Americans

KAREN PRICE HOSSELL

Heinemann Library
Chicago, Illinois

© 2004 Heinemann Library
a division of Reed Elsevier Inc.
Chicago, Illinois

Customer Service 888-454-2279

Visit our website at www.heinemannlibrary.com

Designed by Roslyn Broder
Photo research by Scott Braut
Printed in China by WKT Company Limited

08 07 06 05 04
10 9 8 7 6 5 4 3 2 1

Library of Congress Cataloging-in-Publication Data
Price Hossell, Karen, 1957-
    Pakistani Americans / Karen Price Hossell.
        v. cm. -- (We are America)
    Includes bibliographical references (p) and index.
    Contents: Masooma goes to America -- Pakistan -- Moving to the United States -- Living in the United States -- Pakistani immigration today -- Pakistani Americans across the U.S. -- Everyday life -- Pakistani-American communities -- Festivals and celebrations -- Holidays -- Music and dancing -- Pakistani food -- Masooma today -- Pakistani immigration chart.
    ISBN 1-4034-5023-4
    1. Pakistani Americans--History--Juvenile literature. 2. Pakistani Americans--Social life and customs--Juvenile literature. [1. Pakistani Americans.] I. Title. II. Series.
    E184.P28P75 2004
    973'.04914122--dc22
                                   2003021703

Acknowledgments
The author and publisher are grateful to the following for permission to reproduce copyright material: pp. 4, 5, 28, 29 Courtesy of Masooma Haq; p. 7 K. M. Chaudary/AP Wide World Photos; p. 8 Joseph Sohm/ChromoSohm Inc./Corbis; pp. 9, 22, 24 Spencer Grant/Photo Edit; pp. 10, 14 Tim Boyle/Getty Images; pp. 11, 20, 23, 26 Martha Cooper; p. 12 Gary Conner/Photo Edit; p. 13 Debbie Egan-Chin/Daily News LP; pp. 16, 17 Laura Dwight/Photo Edit; pp. 18, 25 Robert Brenner/Photo Edit; p. 19 Jeff Greenberg/Photo Edit; p. 21 Courtesy of Sheeza Khawar Hussain and Zakir Hussain; p. 27 Renee Comet Photography/StockFood

Cover photographs by Robert Brenner/Photo Edit, (background) Jill Birschbach/Heinemann Library

Special thanks to Mahtalat Abbasi and Faiza Hamayoon for her comments in preparation of this book. The author wishes to thank Brian Krumm and Masooma Haq for sharing her story.

Some quotations and material used in this book come from the following source. In some cases, quotes have been abridged for clarity: p. 10 U.S. Department of State's Office of International Information Programs (usinfo.state.gov) "Pakistani-Americans Talk to Pakistanis about Muslim Life in the U.S." by Susan Domowitz.

A Pakistani-American family at a festival in New York City is shown on the cover of this book. Devon Avenue, a street in Chicago with many Pakistani-American businesses, is shown in the background.

Contents

Some words are shown in bold, **like this.** You can find out what they mean by looking in the glossary.

Masooma Goes to America

In 1973, when Masooma Haq was five years old, she and her family moved from Pakistan to the state of Maine. They had other family members who already lived in Maine. Masooma's parents thought their children would have a better chance at getting a good education in the United States. Like many other Pakistani **immigrants,** Masooma missed living in Pakistan at first. She missed her cousins and aunts and uncles.

This photo shows Masooma, her sister Aysha, and some of their cousins in Lahore, Pakistan. Masooma is the third child from the left and Aysha is on her right.

Some students at her school in Maine made fun of Masooma's name and the food she brought for lunch. But Masooma's teachers asked her questions about herself, her family, and Pakistan. That made her feel more comfortable. After a while, she learned how to speak English and started to make friends. She began to have fun playing with classmates and children who lived in her apartment building.

Masooma is pronounced like this: (ma-SUE-ma). She is about four years old in this photo of her and her father at an airport in Pakistan.

Before I came to the United States, I had heard a lot of stories of how great it was. I remember thinking there are toys that talk and walk and big chocolate bars and Coke. Those things were not as available in Pakistan when I was little.

—Masooma Haq

Pakistan

Pakistan is a country in southern Asia. Pakistan was once part of India, which used to be ruled by Great Britain. When India gained its **independence** in 1947, India was divided according to the country's religious beliefs. Most **Hindus** remained in India, and most **Muslims** moved into two new areas of India's land, East Pakistan or West Pakistan. In 1971, a **civil war** broke out between East and West Pakistan. East Pakistan declared itself a new nation, called Bangladesh. West Pakistan then became known as Pakistan.

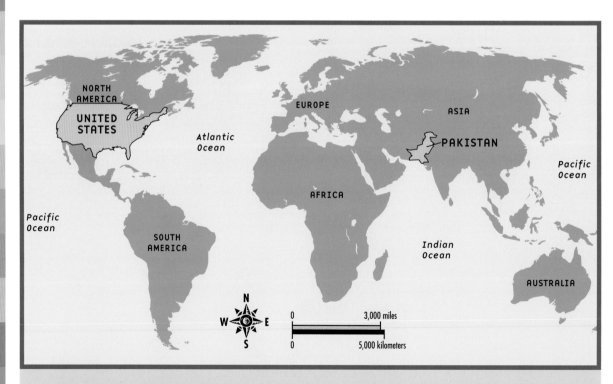

This map shows where Pakistan and the United States are located in the world.

This group of students had class outside their school in Lahore, Pakistan.

About the time of the civil war, many Pakistani people started **immigrating** to the United States to get away from the fighting. A U.S. law passed in 1965 had made it easier for Pakistani people to move to the U.S. Since 1947, the U.S. government had allowed only 105 Pakistanis into the U.S. each year. But after the new law was passed, many more could go to the U.S.

Most of the people who live in Pakistan's countryside are farmers. People who live in the cities work in shops, offices, and factories. In the factories, workers might make sports equipment or medical instruments used by doctors.

Moving to the United States

Until the 1960s, few people had moved from Pakistan to the United States. By the 1970s, many Pakistani **immigrants** had arrived in the U.S. Most of them had been to college and found jobs as **engineers,** doctors, and scientists. Some found jobs as taxi drivers and store clerks. Most Pakistani immigrants **settled** in cities such as New York, Chicago, and Washington, D.C.

Like many other Pakistani Americans, this family settled near Washington, D.C. They moved to Alexandria, Virginia.

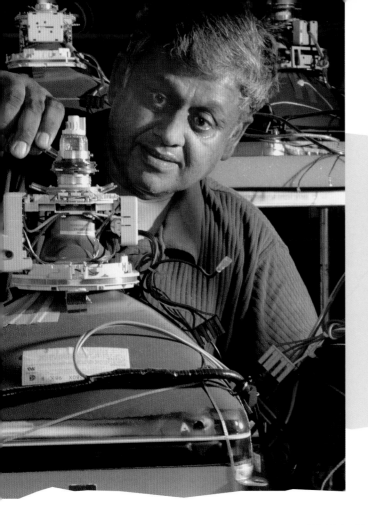

Many Pakistani people settled on the West Coast of the U.S. This Pakistani-American man repairs televisions in Laguna Hills, California.

One reason that most Pakistani immigrants settled in cities was because there were more jobs there. It was also easier to get around because of public transportation, such as trains and buses. Other people from Pakistan also lived in these cities, so the immigrants felt comfortable moving there.

It is easier to follow your dreams in the United States than in any other country in the world . . . You can live your own life, follow your own **traditions**, and pray at any place you want without any trouble.

—Adeel Bhutta, a Pakistani-American student

Living in the United States

Most of the Pakistani **immigrants** who came to the United States in the 1970s and early 1980s were **engineers,** doctors, and pharmacists. They came to the U.S. because they had skills that people in the U.S.

needed and because they could find jobs. Most of the new immigrants **settled** in city neighborhoods where other Pakistani people lived. Many enjoyed talking with and being around other Pakistani people.

An area in Chicago has a large Pakistani and Asian-Indian population. Nuzhat Kazi, a Pakistani American, runs a video store in Chicago.

This Pakistani-American family lives in Brooklyn, New York.

Many of the new immigrants sent money they earned back to family members who still lived in Pakistan. Relatives often used the money to come to the U.S. and settle near them. Family is very important to many Pakistani Americans, and they are often happiest when their entire families are together.

Time Line

1947 India's land is divided into India, East Pakistan, and West Pakistan.

1965 A new U.S. law allows more immigrants from Asia to move to the United States.

1971 During a **civil war** between East Pakistan and West Pakistan, East Pakistan declares itself the new nation of Bangladesh.

2000 More than 40,000 Pakistanis immigrate to the U.S.

Pakistani Immigration Today

Today, people from Pakistan often come to the United States after high school to go to college. Sometimes they plan to go back to Pakistan after college. Many of them end up staying in the U.S. to find jobs. Some states with large populations of Pakistani Americans are New York, California, Texas, and Illinois. More than 15,000 Pakistani Americans live in Illinois.

This woman from Pakistan moved to Westwood, California, to attend college there.

This group of Pakistani Americans met in Brooklyn, New York, on September 21, 2001. They wanted to let other Americans to know that they did not support terrorism in any way.

Pakistani Americans might face more **discrimination** today than those who came to the U.S. earlier. Thousands of Pakistani Americans who lived in New York left the U.S. after September 11, 2001. On that day, **terrorists** crashed airplanes into the World Trade Center towers in New York City and the **Pentagon** in Washington, D.C. Thousands of people died. Many Pakistani Americans were treated unfairly because the terrorists were said to be **Muslims,** like many Pakistani Americans are. Some Pakistani Americans felt very uncomfortable and moved to Canada, Europe, or back to Pakistan.

Pakistani Americans Across the U.S.

The first Pakistani **immigrants** who came to the United States **settled** in many areas of the country. They formed groups to give newcomers from Pakistan information about the U.S. and help them in other ways. There are Pakistani-American **associations** in many states, including Connecticut, Florida, Georgia, and North Carolina. One group that aids Pakistani Americans living in the U.S. and Canada is the Pakistani American Association of North America.

This center in Chicago provided a place for Pakistani Americans to meet other people from Pakistan. They could also get information on how to find jobs and where to live.

This map shows some of the cities and states where Pakistani people first moved to and where many still live today.

Just like other Americans, Pakistani Americans live in many different areas across the U.S., from small towns to big cities. Many of the early Pakistani immigrants have bought homes in the U.S. Some of them have moved out of the cities and into the suburbs, the smaller towns outside of big cities.

Adjusting to the United States was not very difficult. The only problem I faced was the unique and diverse English accent that is spoken here. But with so many English movies and media, it is now only a matter of time before you find yourself at home.

—Adeel Bhutta

Everyday Life

The everyday lives of Pakistani Americans
are very similar to those of other Americans.
They go to school or work, spend time with family
members, and do household chores. There are
some differences, however. For example, some
young Pakistani Americans may go to special
schools where they learn about Islam, the religion
that **Muslims** follow. They also study subjects
that other American students do, like science
and math.

*This Pakistani-American woman is helping her daughter
with her homework.*

Many young Pakistani Americans take care of children and help out around the house. This Pakistani-American girl is baby-sitting and reading to a six-year-old Pakistani girl.

In Pakistan, some children do not get to attend school at all. Some people cannot afford to send their children to school. Pakistani-American children attend schools just as other American children do. Pakistani-American students usually graduate from high school and often attend colleges. Sometimes, Pakistani-American children take over businesses owned by their families after they finish school.

Pakistani-American Communities

Belonging to a **community** is important to many Pakistani Americans. Friends and neighbors in a community are often treated like part of the family. Many Pakistani Americans enjoy living around other Pakistani Americans. Usually, they have the same **traditions** and celebrations and eat the same kinds of food.

*Pakistani Americans celebrate their **culture** and history at festivals held in cities. This Pakistani-American family is shown waving flags from Pakistan and the United States.*

The Statue of Liberty has welcomed millions of immigrants to New York City, such as these Pakistani boys and girls. Thousands of Pakistani Americans live in New York.

There are several large Pakistani-American communities in the United States. Many Pakistani Americans live in New York City and Chicago. About 100,000 Pakistani Americans live in Brooklyn, a part of New York City. Several thousand Pakistani Americans live in the Boston area. More than 20,000 Pakistani Americans live in California. Many Pakistani **immigrants** also live in Houston, Texas.

Festivals and Celebrations

Pakistani Americans organize and take part in some of the same festivals that take place in Pakistan. One such festival is called *Basant,* or Spring Festival. There is a large celebration of this festival in the Pakistani city of Lahore. It is held to celebrate the coming of the spring season. Women and girls wear colorful scarves and clothing. Boys and men compete in kite-flying contests.

Kite-flying contests are part of the Basant *festival in Pakistan. This Pakistani-American man flew a kite in a park in New York City.*

*Zakir Hussain and Sheeza Khawar are both Pakistani Americans.
They met at the college they attended in North Carolina. They were
married in a* **traditional** *Pakistani wedding ceremony in 2000.*

In some ways, Pakistani-American marriage celebrations
are different than other American weddings. The
celebration begins several days before the wedding.
There are also events that are similar to those in other
American weddings. One such event is called the *dholki*.
It is similar to a bride's wedding shower. Family and
friends of the bride gather to spend time with the bride.
They also practice the singing and dancing that will be
part of the wedding celebration.

Holidays

Pakistan **Independence** Day is an important holiday for Pakistani Americans. On August 14, Pakistani Americans remember when Pakistan gained independence from India. In cities such as Augusta, Georgia; Cary, North Carolina; and Lodi, California, there are festivals held to celebrate this day. Pakistani Americans set up booths and sell Pakistani food, clothing, and art. In Chicago, a parade is held to celebrate Pakistan Independence Day. About 15,000 people attended the parade in 2003.

The Pakistani-American girls shown in the photo attended a festival to celebrate Pakistani Independence Day in Fullerton, California.

Many Pakistani Americans are Muslims. These Muslims prayed outside in a park in New York City at the end of the religious holiday called Ramadan.

An important religious holiday for Pakistani Americans is called **Ramadan.** For a month, Pakistani Americans who are **Muslims** do not eat or drink every day from sunrise to sunset. The celebration at the end of Ramadan is called *Eid-ul-Fitr.* People pray and bring gifts to their friends. Seventy days after *Eid-ul-Fitr* is *Eid-ul-Adha,* which is another holy day.

Music and Dancing

Pakistani Americans enjoy many different kinds of music. Pakistani pop musicians often give concerts in cities such as San Francisco and New York City. One kind of popular Pakistani music and dancing is called *bhangra. Bhangra* has been around for hundreds of years. Musicians use drums called *dhol* to play *bhangra.* The drums are worn around the neck and beaten with hands or with drumsticks. The music is fast-paced and fun to dance to.

This crowd enjoyed a concert of Pakistani music at California State University.

These Pakistani-American musicians played drums and other instruments in a parade.

Some Pakistani Americans like to listen to **traditional** Pakistani music called *qawwali. Qawwali* is slower than pop music or *bhangra*. It is sung by one person who repeats the same groups of words over and over. An instrument called the harmonium, which is like a piano, is used in *qawwali*. Two types of drums called the tabla and the *dholak* are also played. A stringed instrument called the *sarangi* is also used in *qawwali*.

Pakistani Food

Pakistani Americans often like to eat Pakistani food. Many other Americans like it, too. Pakistani food is very spicy. Pakistani Americans like to add a red spice made from hot peppers to their food. They use many other spices as well, so their food is very tasty.

This Pakistani-American man served food at a booth near the Pakistani Day Parade in New York City.

This type of bread, called chapatti, is often served with meals of Pakistani food. A glass of chai tea is also shown. It is served at many Pakistani restaurants.

Pakistani cooks use lamb, beef, chicken, and fish in their meals. They make curry, a spicy stew, using meat, vegetables, and spices. With most meals, they serve flat bread called chapatti or roti. The diners tear off pieces of the bread and dip them into curry sauce. Another kind of flat bread is called nan. Chapatti is often cooked in a frying pan, while nan is baked. Rice is often served, as well. A **traditional** drink is *lassi,* which is a drink made with yogurt.

Masooma Today

After she finished high school, Masooma Haq went to college in New York. Then she got a job working in Seattle, Washington, helping teachers in classrooms. Today, she lives in Seattle with her sister and her sister's husband. Masooma is studying to get a **degree** in teaching. In 2004, Masooma went back to Pakistan for the first time since she was five to visit family members who still live there.

Masooma's father took this photo in Seattle just before Masooma entered a college program to earn a degree in teaching.

Masooma is also an artist and sometimes sells her artwork. She also practices Falun Dafa. She is not a **Muslim** like most Pakistani people, although her parents are. Falun Dafa is a Chinese **spiritual practice** that Masooma says is based on truth and being kind to others. Like other **immigrants** in the United States, Masooma appreciates the fact that she has the freedom to follow any spiritual belief she chooses.

Masooma is seen here at her home in Seattle.

What does it mean to be an American? It means having many basic rights that a lot of people do not have. Like the ability to vote, go to school, work, being able to do **human rights** work, and being able to practice my spiritual practice without fear.

—Masooma Haq

Pakistani Immigration Chart

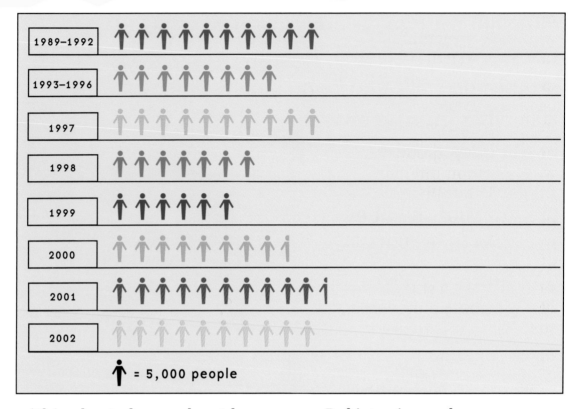

1989–1992	👤👤👤👤👤👤👤👤👤👤
1993–1996	👤👤👤👤👤👤👤👤👤
1997	👤👤👤👤👤👤👤👤👤👤
1998	👤👤👤👤👤👤👤
1999	👤👤👤👤👤👤
2000	👤👤👤👤👤👤👤👤
2001	👤👤👤👤👤👤👤👤👤👤👤
2002	👤👤👤👤👤👤👤👤👤

👤 = 5,000 people

This chart shows about how many Pakistani people moved to the United States from 1989 to 2002.

Source: U.S. Immigration and Naturalization Service

More Books to Read

Black, Carolyn. *Pakistan: The Culture.* New York: Crabtree Publishing, 2002.

Nobleman, Marc Tyler. *Pakistan.* Mankato, Minn.: Capstone Press, 2003.

An older reader can help you with this book:
Khan, Eaniqa, and Rob Unwin. *Pakistan.* Chicago: Raintree, 1998.

Glossary

association group of people who have something in common and work together toward a goal

civil war war fought between people who live in the same country

community group of people with common interests and traditions who live together

culture ideas, skills, arts, and way of life for a certain group of people

degree title a student earns after finishing a program of study at a college or university

discrimination unfair treatment of people because of where they are from, how they look, or what they believe

engineer person who uses scientific knowledge for practical purposes, like building roads or bridges or making electrical tools

Hindu person who follows Hinduism, a major religion in India. Hinduism is based on dharma, which are ways to live life.

human rights things that a person can claim as their own simply because they are human, such as access to food and shelter and freedom from slavery

immigrate to come to a country to live there for a long time. A person who immigrates is an immigrant.

independence condition of being free from the rule of other countries, governments, or people

Muslim person who follows the Islam religion. This religion follows the teachings of the Koran, a holy book.

Pentagon five-sided building in Washington, D.C., that is the headquarters for the U.S. military

Ramadan ninth month of the year during which Muslims do not eat between sunrise and sunset

settle to make a home for yourself and others

spiritual practice way of living, similar to a religion, that people use to guide them through life and behavior

terrorist person who uses violent acts to try to force a government or political group to give in to their demands

tradition belief or practice handed down through the years from one generation to the next

Index